Knut

How One Little Polar Bear Captivated the World

Told by **Juliana, Isabella,** and **Craig Hatkoff** and **Dr. Gerald R. Uhlich**

SCHOLASTIC PRESS • NEW YORK

We would like to thank Thomas Dörflein and André Schüle for their enormous personal commitment to raising Knut, as well as everyone at Zoo Berlin who contributed to the effort. We are also grateful to Lauren Thompson for her contribution in making this book, and to Robert Buchanan and Barbara Nielsen of Polar Bears International for their careful reading of the manuscript.

Pronunciation Guide to German Names and Terms

Knut | K'-noot

Thomas Dörflein | Toe-mas Dor-fline

André Schüle | Ahn-dray Shoo-luh

Eisbärbaby | Ice-bear-bay-bee ("polar bear cub")

Nein! | Nine! ("No!")

Komm! | Kohm! ("Come!")

Text © 2007 by Turtle Pond Publications, LLC and Zoologischer Garten Berlin AG

Compilation of text and photographs © 2007 by Turtle Pond Publications, LLC and Zoologischer Garten Berlin AG

Photos pages 7, 10, 13, 14, 15, 16, 17, 18, 19, 21, 27, 30, 32 © 2006, 2007 Zoo Berlin / Peter Griesbach; photo page 20 © 2007 Zoo Berlin / André Schüle; photos pages 4, 22, 28 © Sean Gallup/Getty Images; photo page 8 © Rainer Jensen/epa/Corbis; photo page 23 © Arnd Wiegmann/ Reuters/Corbis; photos pages 24, 29 © Andreas Rentz/Getty Images; photos pages 25, 26 © Marcus Brandt/AFP/Getty Images; photo page 31 © John Macdougall/AFP/Getty Images; photo page 34 © Hinrich Baesemann/dpa/Corbis

Library of Congress Cataloging-in-Publication Data

Knut : how one little polar bear captivated the world / told by Isabella, Juliana, and Craig Hatkoff, and Gerald R. Uhlich ; with photographs by Zoo Berlin.

p. cm.

ISBN-13: 978-0-545-04716-6 (hardcover)
ISBN-10: 0-545-04716-1 (hardcover)

UK ISBN-13: 978-1-407106-00-7
UK ISBN-10: 1-407-10600-7

1. Knut (Polar bear)—Juvenile literature. 2. Polar bear—Germany—Berlin—Biography—Juvenile literature. 3. Zoo animals—Germany—Berlin—Biography—Juvenile literature. 4. Zoologischer Garten (Berlin, Germany)—Juvenile literature. I. Hatkoff, Isabella. II. Zoologischer Garten (Berlin, Germany)

SF408.6.P64K68 2007
599.786092'9—dc22
2007021379

10 9 8 7 6 5 4 3 2 1   07 08 09 10 11
Printed in Mexico   49
First Edition, November 2007
Book design by Becky Terhune

RESPECT HABITATS. KNUT

Dear Friends,

I had the great fortune recently to coauthor with my young daughter Isabella the true story of Owen, an orphaned baby hippo in Kenya who was raised by a giant tortoise named Mzee after the Asian tsunami. When our family heard about another orphan, Knut, the world's cutest polar bear, Isabella and I, joined by my eldest daughter, Juliana, thought we should tell his story, too. Knut had survived through the perseverance not only of a zookeeper named Thomas Dörflein, but also an entire community at Zoo Berlin — a timely environmental metaphor of Man helping Animal to survive. How beautiful!

As Knut's story and the amazing photographs of him circled the globe, Knut became, almost overnight, an international symbol of environmental responsibility. As people fell in love with Knut, it seemed that one little polar bear could help "de-polarize" the hotly debated issue of global warming. In a world where polar bear habitats are rapidly shrinking, Knut reminds us just what we are at risk of losing. He makes it clear that we all breathe the same air at one point or another and encourages us to respect all habitats. In telling Knut's story, perhaps his grandchildren might just be remembered as the descendants of the little cub who made a difference in the world.

Craig Hatkoff

Juliana Hatkoff

Isabella Hatkoff

One December afternoon, in a cozy, dark enclosure in a zoo in Berlin, Germany, a polar bear cub was born. He was so small that a child could easily have cradled him. His eyes were closed tight, and his pink skin showed through his fine, white fur. He was just a tiny polar bear cub, but he would soon be loved by millions of people around the world.

His name is Knut, and this is his story.

Knut (pronounced K'-noot) was born on December 5, 2006, at Zoo Berlin, one of the world's largest and most respected zoos. Thomas Dörflein, the chief bear keeper, and André Schüle, one of the veterinarians, were on hand when Knut's mother, Tosca, gave birth to two healthy cub brothers. But Thomas and André were anxious. Wild animal mothers don't always know how to take care of their babies. If Tosca wasn't able to be the cubs' mother, Thomas and André would have to try to hand-raise them. Thomas and André watched Tosca carefully, but she showed little interest in the cubs. So after five hours, Thomas carefully gathered them up and rushed them to the small room that would be their first home.

The cubs were placed in an incubator, a small, heated bed. As they hungrily drank their first meal from baby bottles, a new life began for Thomas. He was to devote the next few months to being an around-the-clock foster father.

Snow dens in the wild get very warm — up to 95 degrees Fahrenheit — so Thomas was careful to keep Knut toasty.

The cubs were not given names at first, because it is not unusual for newborn animals to survive only a few days. And unfortunately, on the fourth day, one of the cubs suddenly developed a high fever. Within a few hours, he died. It was a very sad loss. But Thomas and André knew that they had done all they could. Now they focused all their care on the remaining baby.

André checked on the cub several times a day, but it was Thomas who saw to the cub's every need. The cub could drink only about four tablespoons of formula milk at one time. After just two hours, he would yelp in hunger again. Day and night, Thomas would boil water, mix the formula, give the cub his bottle, and settle him back down in the incubator. He also had to clean the cub's bedding and sterilize the bottles. Thomas napped when he could.

It was an exhausting routine. But Thomas was determined to give this cub the best possible chance at survival. He even moved a bed and sleeping bag into the cub's room so that he could always be nearby.

Mother polar bears groom and nuzzle their cubs a lot, and Thomas was happy to stroke and comfort Knut all he needed.

Week after week, the cub's fur grew in more thickly, his tummy got plumper, and his body got stronger. With his bright black eyes he looked around at everything. Until the cub was four weeks old, Thomas continued to feed him every two hours. He also bathed him, brushed him, and rubbed him with baby oil each day. He even played Elvis songs on the guitar for him. Thomas was very, very tired from the endless work, but he came to love the cub as if he were his own baby. And the cub thrived.

The tiny bear became the center of Thomas's life. But he missed his own family at home: his partner, Daniela, and her five-year-old son, Sylvester. They missed him, too. But they felt very proud of him. They visited Thomas every day. And on Christmas Eve, they arrived with a special dinner, presents, and even a beautifully decorated tree. Their love helped to keep Thomas's spirits up.

Finally, when the cub was thirty-two days old, Thomas decided it was time to give him a permanent name. To Thomas, the cub just looked like a "Knut" — and so Knut it was.

Even when they are little, polar bears have big paws.

Before Knut was born, Thomas had hand-raised a brown bear cub and a wolf pup.

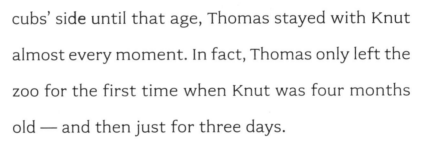

Thomas and André used their expert knowledge about polar bears to take good care of Knut. When Knut outgrew his incubator, they built a wooden sleeping box for him that was the same size as a mother bear's den — about as big as a very large toy chest. They kept the room dark and warm, since polar bear cubs don't leave their den and don't experience bright light or cold until they are almost three months old. And because mother bears stay by their cubs' side until that age, Thomas stayed with Knut almost every moment. In fact, Thomas only left the zoo for the first time when Knut was four months old — and then just for three days.

Meanwhile, Knut already had thousands of friends outside the zoo. The people of Berlin, and soon all of Germany, fell in love with "Eisbärbaby Knut" and his foster father, Thomas. They were eager to visit Knut at the zoo, but his keepers felt that Knut was still too young to appear in public.

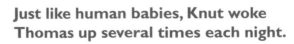

Just like human babies, Knut woke Thomas up several times each night.

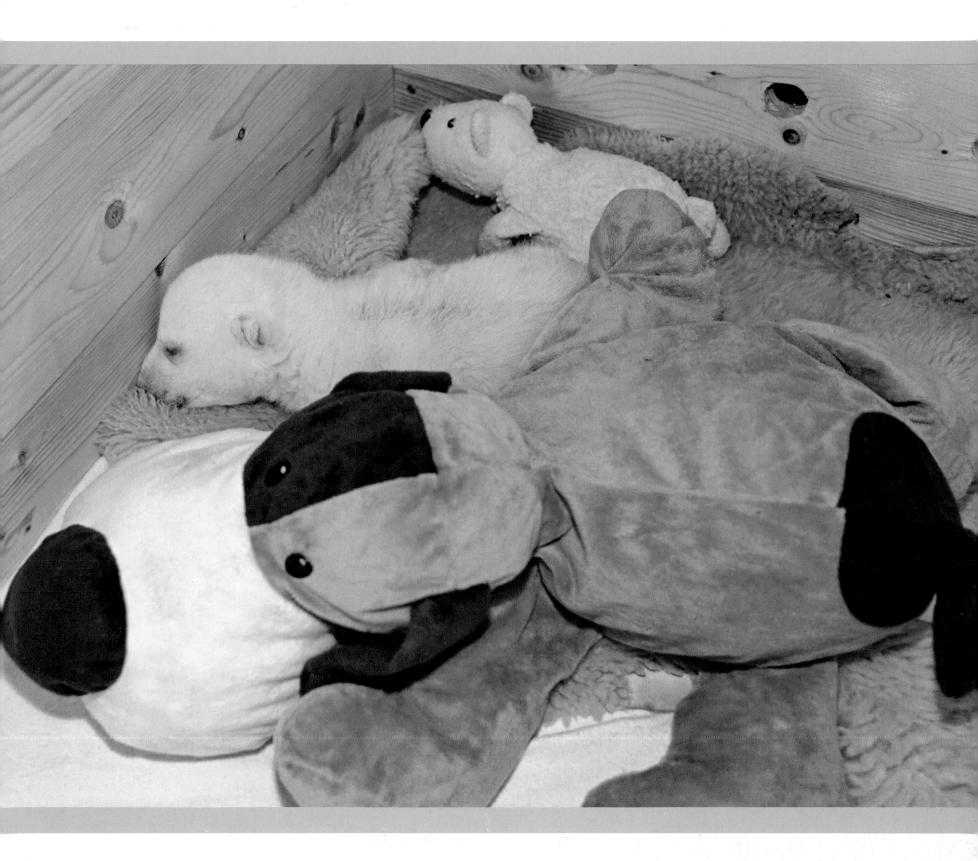

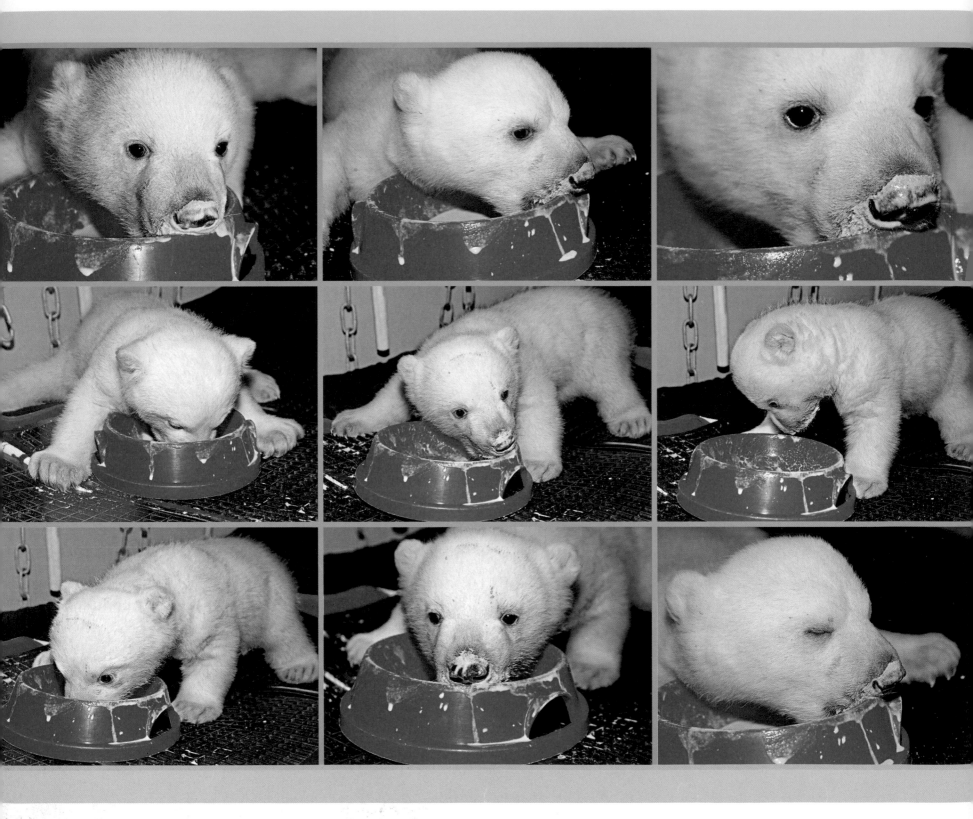

Knut eagerly laps up his puppy-formula milk mixed with cat food, corn syrup, and cod liver oil.

By the time Knut was ready to move to his sleeping box, he was strong enough to pull himself along with his front legs. He already loved to tussle with his stuffed animals or blanket. A month later, he took his first wobbly steps on all four paws. A week after that, he had his first meal of milk, with a bit of kitten food mixed in, from a bowl. Thomas and André laughed as most of the food ended up on Knut's fur and the floor, and very little ended up inside Knut. But he certainly enjoyed it. After that, Knut had his first bath in a small tub. He enjoyed that, too. For Knut, every activity is a chance to wrestle, pounce, and play.

Bathtime for Knut!

On a warm day in March, when Knut was three months old, Thomas led him outdoors for the first time. Knut excitedly explored every corner of the small play area, but he never strayed far from Thomas. In the sandbox, Knut made two discoveries: one, that sand is not good to eat, and, two, that sand is great fun to roll around in. When he shook out his fur, sand flew everywhere.

For Thomas, raising Knut has been very rewarding, but it isn't always easy. One night, Knut climbed out of his sleeping box and awoke Thomas by pouncing on his head. It was the first time that Knut had climbed out on his own. After that, Thomas made sure to close the sleeping box at night. Knut sometimes shows his affection for Thomas by pulling hard on his hair. Thomas lets Knut know that he prefers when Knut licks his face or nuzzles with him, nose to nose, in a friendly polar bear-style greeting.

Playing can wear Knut out.

Finally the keepers decided that Knut was strong and healthy enough to be viewed by zoo visitors. They announced that, on March 23, Knut and Thomas would appear in public for two hours. Then, a week before the big day, a newspaper reported one man's comments that Knut should not have been rescued after his mother rejected him, because in the wild a cub would not have been rescued. Knut's fans were shocked. People all over Germany spoke up in support for Knut, Thomas, and Zoo Berlin. News of the man's statement and the public's strong reaction against it quickly spread around the world. Suddenly, Knut was an international celebrity.

Knut may be little, but he moves fast.

Thousands of Knut admirers streamed into the zoo the morning of March 23. Almost five hundred journalists, including camera crews from a hundred television stations, arrived to report on Knut's first public appearance. There were reporters and visitors from places as far away as Canada, Colombia, Pakistan, Japan, and New Zealand. And when Thomas and Knut stepped out into the enclosure, the crowd cheered as if they were movie stars.

For Thomas, who is rather shy, all this fame was quite surprising. But he did his best to give all his attention to Knut. And all Knut wanted to do was play. So with Knut's favorite green blanket, Thomas and Knut played tug-of-war. Then Knut clambered on the rocks and wrestled with his ball. He charmed everyone.

Day after day, huge crowds came to admire Knut as he played with his keepers and his sticks, balls, and teddy bears. As people's love for Knut grew, many thought about Knut's polar bear cousins in the wild. With temperatures rising around the globe, the icy regions where polar bears live are shrinking. Some scientists even believe that polar bears could become extinct during our lifetime. Many of Knut's new friends realized what the world might lose and started to ask what they could do to help.

After rolling in sand, Knut looks more like a brown bear than a polar bear!

When Knut was teething, Thomas spent the
night next to Knut in his box to comfort him.

With his cute waddle and playful spirit, it was hard not to love
Knut. He received as many as two hundred letters each week. People
of all ages sent poems and other words of friendship. Children who
were too young to write drew pictures for Knut. Everyone wanted
Knut to know how happy he made them feel.

One day, visitors worried when, rather than playing, Knut lay on
the ground, holding his paws over his eyes or on his swollen cheek.
Over the next few days, Knut and Thomas didn't make their usual
public appearances. Was Knut sick? It turned out that because
Knut's permanent teeth were coming in, his mouth was sore.
Thomas helped Knut feel better by rubbing his gums and by letting
Knut cuddle with him when he slept. Before
long, Knut was back, as lively and full of fun
as ever.

Knut and Thomas exchange
a polar bear kiss.

Thomas's favorite times with Knut happen away from the crowds. Every morning, before the zoo opens, Thomas leads Knut on a walk through the zoo grounds. It was during these early morning walks that Thomas gave Knut his first swimming lessons. Knut already enjoyed wading in shallow water. But when Thomas dove into deep water and called to Knut to follow him, Knut hesitated. Thomas patiently encouraged him until Knut finally jumped in. Before long, Knut was swimming around in polar bear fashion, paddling with his front legs and using his back legs to steer.

Just as a bear mother would, Thomas makes sure that Knut's boisterous energy doesn't get out of hand. If Knut grows impatient before a feeding and starts to nip, Thomas will warn him, "Nein, nein!" ("No, no!"), until Knut stops. Usually, Knut listens well. When Thomas calls, "Knut, komm!" ("Knut, come!"), Knut always comes running.

When Knut misbehaves, Thomas gently but firmly corrects him.

Knut will play with anything.

Every day, Knut is growing bigger and stronger. By the time Knut is a year old, he will be so big that he could hurt Thomas without meaning to. It might not be safe for them to play. Thomas and Knut will be together as long as they can. And no matter what, Thomas will stay closely involved in Knut's care until Knut is ready to be independent. Adult polar bears spend most of their time alone, so Knut won't be lonely if it happens that Thomas can no longer be with him every day. And Knut will always be very special to Thomas.

Knut's favorite place to be is close to Thomas.

And that's the story of Knut, who survived and thrived because of the love and care of his foster father, Thomas, and the support of Zoo Berlin. Knut has brought joy to millions around the world, but more importantly, he has reminded us that one small creature can make a big difference. Knut may be just a tiny polar bear cub, but he inspires us to do everything we can to help polar bears in the wild. Together, we can take small actions that will lead to big change. If we all do our part to help save the polar bears' natural habitat — and all natural habitats — we will give Knut's story a very happy ending indeed.

MORE ABOUT POLAR BEARS . . .

How They Look

Polar bears are perfectly built to keep cozy in freezing weather. They have thick fur covering their entire bodies, except the tips of their noses and the bottoms of their paws. This yellowish-white coat helps them blend in with the snow and ice around them. Underneath the fur is more protection against the cold: a layer of blubber, or fat, that is three to four inches thick. Small ears and a short tail also help prevent heat loss. Giant, partly webbed paws are just right for walking across slippery ice or swimming through cold water.

Grown-up polar bears are much bigger than baby Knut. Females weigh between 300 and 700 pounds, and males weigh between 700 and 1,600 pounds — about three times as much as a lion!

What They Eat

Polar bears like to eat meat, especially fatty meat. They need to consume an average of about four and a half pounds of fat every day in order to survive. In the wild, their main source of food is seals. Instead of trying to hunt out at sea, they wait patiently at openings in sea ice — sheets of ice on top of seawater — because this is where seals come up to breathe. They can smell a seal from ten football fields away and under three feet of ice. Their sense of smell is so good that some people call polar bears "noses with legs."

Family Time

Unlike other bears, polar bears do not hibernate. Only new mothers and their babies spend long periods of time in dens. A pregnant female scrapes a tunnel in the snow and makes a dark, quiet chamber where she cuddles up to give birth. A litter typically includes between one and three cubs, and the mother lives with the cubs in the den for three to five months. During that time, she does not eat any food, surviving only on her fat reserves. Mothers stay with their cubs for between one and three years, until they are able to hunt for themselves.

Where They Live

Polar bears make their homes in large open spaces around the Arctic. They roam from Alaska to Russia, and from Canada to Greenland. There are no polar bears in the Southern Hemisphere.

The Latin name for polar bears is *Ursus maritimus,* which means "sea bear." It's a name that suits polar bears because they spend so much time in the water. They love to swim. Sometimes they wander off the coast on drifting packs of ice called ice floes. Polar bears spend most of their time on sea ice — because it's the best place to hunt seals.

THE BIGGEST THREAT TO POLAR BEARS

Polar bears in the wild do not have natural predators. Most scientists agree that the biggest threat to polar bears is global warming: changing weather caused by gases produced when we do things like drive cars and burn coal. These gases trap sunlight in the earth's atmosphere, which makes temperatures rise on the surface of the earth and in the oceans.

Studies show that permanent ice in the Arctic has dropped by 9.8% every ten years since 1978. Ice is melting in the spring earlier than it used to, and freezing later in fall. This means that polar bears' hunting areas are shrinking, and their hunting season is getting shorter.

Although nobody knows exactly how many polar bears live in the wild, researchers have counted fewer bears and cubs in recent years. As hunting has become more difficult for polar bears, people have also noticed the bears are not as big as they used to be. Experts in Canada found that male bears weigh 150 pounds less now than they did thirty years ago. Some scientists say that if warming trends continue at their current pace, polar bears could be extinct in our lifetime.

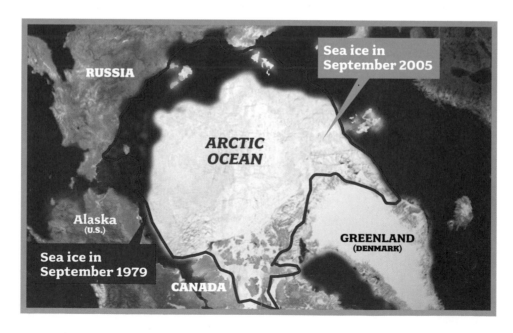

The Arctic's shrinking sea ice.

HOW YOU CAN HELP

There is still time to stop global warming, and you and your friends and family can help. Here are some simple things you can do to keep polar bears safe:

- **Learn more** — Go to www.respect-habitats-knut.org to read about Zoo Berlin's program to help protect the environment.

- **Ride your bike or walk** — Instead of riding in a car, take buses or trains, or use your own legs! When you need to drive, carpool with your friends.

- **Reduce, Reuse, Recycle** — Reuse your water bottles, write on the back side of paper, and always recycle.

- **Plant a tree** — Trees help reduce the amount of harmful gases in the air.

- **Be energy-smart** — Turn off the lights when you leave a room. Ask your parents to turn down the heat in winter, and open windows instead of using air-conditioning in the summer.

- **Speak up!** — Talk to your friends, family, and teachers about global warming. Together, we can help protect the environment — for each other, and for polar bears like Knut.

Selected Sources

Polar Bears International. www.polarbearsinternational.org

U.S. Environmental Protection Agency. http://www.epa.gov/climatechange/

"Arctic Sea Ice Melting Faster, a Study Finds" by Andrew C. Revkin. *The New York Times*, May 1, 2007.

"Feeling the Heat" by Kathryn R. Satterfield. *Time for Kids*, Jan 12, 2007.

"Polar Bear," *Encyclopedia Americana*, Grolier Online, May 4, 2007.